TABLE OF CONTENTS

Executive Summary

In homes, schools, and libraries across the nation, the Internet has become a valuable and even critical tool for our children's success. Access to the Internet furnishes children with new resources with which to learn, new avenues for expression, and new skills to obtain quality jobs.

Our children's access to the Internet, however, can put them in contact with inappropriate and potentially harmful material. Some children inadvertently confront pornography, indecent material, hate sites, and sites promoting violence, while other children actively seek out inappropriate content. Additionally, through participation in chat rooms and other interactive dialogues over the Internet, children can be vulnerable to online predators.

Parents and educators have access to a variety of tools that can help protect children from these dangers. In October 2000, Congress passed the Children's Internet Protection Act (CIPA), which requires schools and libraries that receive federal funds for discounted telecommunications, Internet access, or internal connections services to adopt an Internet safety policy and employ technological protections that block or filter certain visual depictions deemed obscene, pornographic, or harmful to minors.[1] Congress also requested the Department of Commerce's National Telecommunications and Information Administration (NTIA) to (1) evaluate whether the technology measures currently available adequately address the needs of educational institutions, and (2) evaluate the development and effectiveness of local Internet safety policies. Congress also invited any recommendations from NTIA as to how to foster the development of measures that meet these needs. This report sets forth NTIA's public outreach, including comments received through a Request for Comment, its evaluation, and recommendations.

With respect to whether the technology measures currently available address the needs of educational institutions, the commenters identified the following needs of educational institutions:

- balancing the importance of allowing children to use the Internet with the importance of protecting children from inappropriate material;
- accessing online educational materials with a minimum level of relevant content being blocked;
- deciding on the local level how best to protect children from Internet dangers;
- understanding how to fully utilize Internet protection technology measures;
- considering a variety of technical, educational, and economic factors when selecting technology protection measures; and
- adopting an Internet safety strategy that includes technology, human monitoring, and education.

---

[1] Children's Internet Protection Act (CIPA), Pub. L. No. 106-554 (2000) (codified at 20 U.S.C. §§ 6801, 6777, 9134 (2003); 47 U.S.C. § 254 (2003)).

Based on a review of the comments, currently available technology measures have the capacity to meet most, if not all, of these needs and concerns.

Accordingly, NTIA makes the following two recommendations to Congress on how to foster the use of technology protection measures to better meet the needs of educational institutions:

- Technology vendors should offer training services to educational institutions on the specific features of their products.

- CIPA's definition of "technology protection measure" should be expanded to include more than just blocking and filtering technology in order to encompass a vast array of current technological measures that protect children from inappropriate content.

Finally, commenters expressed a great deal of satisfaction regarding the development and effectiveness of Internet safety policies. Specifically, they praise the ability to customize these policies to address the concerns of individual communities. Based on the comments, NTIA has identified best practices for use in developing Internet safety policies.

I.   Introduction

In October 2000, Congress passed the Children's Internet Protection Act (CIPA) as part of the Consolidated Appropriations Act of 2001.[2] CIPA requires schools and libraries receiving discounted telecommunications, Internet access, or internal connections services through federal funding mechanisms to certify and adopt an Internet safety policy and employ technological protections that block or filter certain visual depictions deemed obscene, pornographic, or harmful to minors. Section 1703 of CIPA requests that the National Telecommunications and Information Administration (NTIA) within the U.S. Department of Commerce evaluate the effectiveness of Internet technology protection measures and safety policies to fulfill the needs of educational institutions, make recommendations on fostering the development of measures that meet these needs, and evaluate the development and effectiveness of local Internet safety policies. In accordance with the statute, NTIA initiated a notice and comment proceeding to obtain public comment on these issues.

A.   Children and the Internet

The explosive growth of Internet use in the United States has been fueled in part by children's and teenagers' online activities. Children and teenagers use computers and the Internet more than any other age group.[3] By the fall of 2001, 99 percent of public schools in the United States had access to the Internet, and public schools had expanded Internet access into 87 percent of instructional rooms.[4] Approximately 65 percent of American children ages 2-17 use the Internet from home, school, or other locations.[5]

Access to the resources of the Internet has given children new research tools, information sources, avenues of expression, collaborative learning opportunities, and connections to other communities, among other benefits.[6] But it also has potentially exposed them to the unseemly side of the Internet – indecent material, pornography, hate sites, violent sites, and online predators.[7]

---

[2] CIPA, *supra* note 1.

[3] U.S. Department of Commerce, National Telecommunications and Information Administration, *A Nation Online: How Americans Are Expanding Their Use of the Internet* at 1, 13 (Feb. 2002), *available at* http://www.ntia.doc.gov/ntiahome/dn/index.html.

[4] National Center for Education Statistics, *Internet Access in U.S. Public Schools and Classrooms: 1994-2001* at 3 (September 2002) *available at* http://nces.ed.gov/pubs2002/2002018.pdf.

[5] Corporation for Public Broadcasting, *Connected to the Future* (March 2003).

[6] *See, e.g.,* U.S. Department of Commerce, National Telecommunications and Information Administration, *How Access Benefits Children: Connecting Our Kids to the World of Information* (Sept. 1999).

[7] *The Commission on Child Online Protection Act Final Report to Congress* at 1 (Oct. 20, 2001).

In August 2002, the National Academies released *Youth, Pornography, and the Internet*, a report that studied tools and strategies for protecting children from online pornography. The report concluded that there are no "foreseeable technological 'silver bullets' or single permanent solutions" to keeping children safe from such material.[8] Rather, the report supported solutions that balance the potential benefits of the Internet to children with the competing goals and values of the community.[9]

As the dangers to children in an online environment have emerged, so have a variety of technology tools. Some common technologies used to protect children include:[10]

- Filtering with Yes or No lists:
  - Server-side filtering: Internet service providers and online server software offer filtering techniques to clients that deny access to particular content sources that have been pre-selected for blocking via automated processes, human review, and/or user options. The list of blocked URLs may or may not be disclosed and is regularly updated at the server level.[11]
  - Client-side filtering: This technology prohibits the browser from downloading content based on specified content sources identified by the user. Blocked sites may originate from both the software supplier and/or from the user's decision. Users maintain control over these lists with a password and may periodically download updated lists from the software's website. Some software filters out email or instant messaging.[12]
- Filtering using text-based content analysis: This technology combines PC-based software and server software to conduct real time analysis of a website's content to filter out illicit content. Some software analyzes email and attachments. The user may or may not gain access to how such content is excluded.[13]
- Monitoring and time-limiting technologies: This technology tracks a child's online activities and sets limits on the amount of time a child may spend online. Monitoring software often covers the Internet, email, and instant messaging activities.[14]

---

[8] National Research Council, *Youth, Pornography, and the Internet, Committee to Study Tools and Strategies for Protecting Kids from Pornography and Their Applicability to Other Inappropriate Internet Content* at 387 (May 2002).

[9] *Id.*

[10] *The Commission on Child Online Protection Act Final Report to Congress* (Oct. 20, 2001).

[11] *Id.* at 19.

[12] *Id.* at 21.

[13] *Id.* at 22.

[14] *Id.* at 34.

- Age Verification System: This technology uses an independently-issued ID and controls the flow of online content by conditioning access to a web page with use of a password issued (by a third party) to an adult.[15]

Even the most sophisticated and current technology tools are not one hundred percent effective.[16] Public awareness campaigns and workshops have sought to supplement technology tools.[17] In addition, Congress introduced several bills to legislate a solution.

B.   Congressional Efforts to Protect Children from Inappropriate Online Content

In 1996, Congress first attempted to curb inappropriate online content by passing the Communications Decency Act (CDA).[18] The CDA prohibited the sending or posting of obscene or indecent material via the Internet to persons under the age of 18. The Supreme Court declared the law unconstitutional, however, stating that the law violated free speech under the First Amendment.[19] Specifically, the Court ruled that CDA's vague provisions chilled free speech unknown to the speaker generating the content, and that the CDA's provisions criminalized legitimate, protected speech, including sexually explicit indecent speech, in addition to unprotected obscene speech.

Congress responded by passing the Child Online Protection Act (COPA) of 1998, a law written more narrowly to protect children from inappropriate online content.[20] COPA prohibited commercial web sites from displaying "harmful to minors" material and imposed criminal penalties on violators. A three-judge panel for the United States District Court for the Eastern District of Pennsylvania ruled that COPA's reference to "contemporary community standards" violated the First Amendment when applied to the World Wide Web, and imposed an injunction on the enforcement of COPA.[21] The Third Circuit affirmed this decision stating that the reference to community standards in the definition of "material that is harmful to minors" resulted in an overbroad statute.[22] In May 2002, the Supreme Court vacated the Third Circuit

---

[15] *Id*. at 25-26.

[16] *See Digital Chaperones for Kids: Which Internet Filters Protect the Best? Which Get in the Way?* Consumer Reports, Mar. 2001, at 2.

[17] *See, e.g.,* www.GetNetWise.org and www.NetSmart.org.

[18] The Communications Decency Act of 1996, Pub. L. No. 104-104, 110 Stat. 56 (codified at 47 U.S.C. § 223)(2003)).

[19] Reno v. American Civil Liberties Union, 521 U.S. 844 (1997).

[20] Child Online Protection Act (COPA), Pub. L. No. 105-277, 112 Stat. 2681- 736 (codified at 47 U.S.C. § 231)(2003)).

[21] The American Civil Liberties Union v. Reno, 31 F.Supp. 2d. 473 (E.D. Pa. 1999).

[22] The American Civil Liberties Union v. Reno, 217 F.3d 162 (3d Cir. 1999).

decision and remanded the case for further review.[23] The Court found that "contemporary community standards" by itself does not render the statute overbroad for purposes of the First Amendment.[24] On remand, the Third Circuit found that COPA is not sufficiently narrowly tailored to satisfy the First Amendment requirements.[25]

In October 2000, Congress passed the Children's Internet Protection Act (CIPA) of 2000.[26] The law conditions the receipt of certain federal funding on educational institutions' adoption of technological protections and Internet safety policies. Sections 1712 and 1721 of CIPA, involving the use of filtered Internet access on public computers in libraries, were challenged in court as unconstitutional.[27] In May 2002, the United States District Court for the Eastern District of Pennsylvania struck down these provisions of CIPA as unconstitutional, stating that a technology's tendency to overblock material prohibits the flow of protected speech to library patrons.[28] Under a provision within CIPA, providing for a fast-track appeals process requiring any appeals to be heard by the Supreme Court, the Justice Department appealed the court's decision to the Supreme Court. The Court agreed to review CIPA and heard oral arguments in March 2003.[29]

In a plurality decision, the Supreme Court reversed the District Court's decision in June 2003, finding that the filtering provisions did not violate the First Amendment.[30] Four justices held that (1) the Internet access provided by libraries is not a public forum, and therefore, decisions to block pornography are not subject to heightened scrutiny; (2) the disabling provision eases fears of "overblocking;" and (3) requiring filtering and blocking technology is an appropriate condition on the receipt of federal funding because libraries already exclude pornographic material from their other collections. The Supreme Court underscored "the ease with which patrons may have the filtering software disabled."[31] The Federal Communications

---

[23] Ashcroft v. The American Civil Liberties Union, 535 U.S. 564 (2002).

[24] *Id.* at 566.

[25] The American Civil Liberties Union v. Ashcroft, 322 F.3d 240 (3d Cir. 2003) (holding that the terms "material harmful to minors" and "for commercial purpose," as defined, were not sufficiently narrowly tailored).

[26] CIPA, *supra* note 1.

[27] *See* American Library Association v. United States, No. 01-CV-1303 (E.D. Pa. March 20, 2001); Multnomah County Public Library v. United States, No. 01-CV-1332 (E.D. Pa. March 20, 2001).

[28] American Library Association v. United States, 201 F. Supp. 2d. 401 (E.D. Pa. 2002).

[29] United States v. American Library Association, 123 S. Ct. 551 (2002).

[30] United States v. American Library Association, 123 S. Ct. 2297 (2003).

[31] *Id.*

Commission subsequently issued an order to ensure that its implementation of CIPA complies with the Supreme Court's decision.[32]

C.   NTIA's Evaluation of Technology Protection Measures and Internet Safety Policies

Section 1703(a) of CIPA requests NTIA to initiate a notice and comment proceeding to determine whether currently available blocking and filtering technologies adequately address the needs of educational institutions, to make recommendations on how to foster the development of technologies that meet the needs of schools and libraries, and to evaluate current Internet safety policies. Section 1703(a) of CIPA specifically provides the following:

Sec. 1703. Study of Technology Protection Measures

(a) IN GENERAL. - Not later than 18 months after the date of the enactment of this Act, the National Telecommunications and Information Administration shall initiate a notice and comment proceeding for purposes of ---
> 1) evaluating whether or not currently available technology protection measures, including commercial Internet blocking and filtering software, adequately address the needs of educational institutions;
> (2) making recommendations on how to foster the development of measures that meet such needs; and
> (3) evaluating the development and effectiveness of local Internet safety policies that are currently in operation after community input.

On May 24, 2002, NTIA published a "Request for Comment" in the *Federal Register*,[33] eliciting information about technology protection measures and Internet safety policies. NTIA requested interested parties to submit written comments on any issue of fact, law, or policy germane to the evaluation. NTIA also encouraged commenters to submit copies of relevant studies, surveys, research, or other empirical data. NTIA did not seek comment on the constitutionality of the statute or its provisions. In order to generate a wide range of responses, NTIA conducted extensive outreach to the education community, technology developers, consumer groups, and academia. The "Request for Comment" elicited 42 comments from associations, technology vendors, governmental agencies, academics/university professors, schools, and libraries.[34]

---

[32] *See In the Matter of Federal-State Joint Board on Universal Service, Children's Internet Protection Act*, CC Docket No. 96-45, Order, FCC 03-188 (rel. July 24, 2003) (implementation timing modifications).

[33] Request for Comment on the Effectiveness of Internet Protection Measures and Safety Policies, 67 Fed. Reg. 37396 (May 24, 2002).

[34] *See* Appendix II for list of commenters. *See* www.ntia.doc.gov/ntiahome/ntiageneral/cipacomments/index html for copies of all comments. Comments are also on file at the National Telecommunications and Information Administration. Page numbers refer to the location in the comments on file at NTIA.

II. Evaluation of Existing Technology Protection Measures' Ability to Meet the Needs of Educational Institutions

Section 1703 of CIPA requests that NTIA evaluate whether currently available technology protection measures, including commercial Internet blocking and filtering software, adequately address the needs of educational institutions. In answering this inquiry, the commenters identified six needs of educational institutions:

1) balancing the importance of allowing children to use the Internet with the importance of protecting children from inappropriate material;
2) accessing online educational materials with a minimum level of relevant content being blocked;
3) deciding on the local level how best to protect children from Internet dangers;
4) understanding how to fully utilize Internet protection technology measures;
5) considering a variety of technical, educational, and economic factors when selecting technology protection measures; and
6) adopting an Internet safety strategy that includes technology, human monitoring, and education.

Below we examine these needs and set forth the commenters' evaluation of whether existing technology protection measures are meeting each of these needs.

A. Balancing the Importance of Allowing Children to Use the Internet with the Importance of Protecting Children From Inappropriate Material.

Congress passed CIPA to protect children from inappropriate and harmful content while accessing the Internet at educational institutions that use federal funds.[35] Commenters expressed little doubt that technology plays a role in reducing a child's exposure to inappropriate content.[36] Many commenters wrote of their use of technology protection measures. Several comments from schools and libraries reported using Internet-content filters in order to assist in a safer Internet experience. Some institutions install filters specifically on Internet stations for children under eighteen.[37] Some schools reported the effective use of filtering software. For example, St. Pius X School in Urbandale, Iowa reported using firewall filtering as well as customizable blocking to meet its protection needs. The school's administrators select sites and domains to

---

[35] CIPA, *supra* note 1.

[36] Comment by Center for Democracy and Technology at 5 (no date) [hereinafter CDT]; Comment by Leo Mosier at 1 (Aug. 13, 2002); Comment by Melora Ranney, Charles M. Bailey Public Library at 1 (Aug. 10, 2002) [hereinafter Ranney]; Comment by Cathy Bosley, Fort Morgan Public Library, Fort Morgan, CO at 1 (Aug. 10, 2002) [hereinafter Bosley]; Comment by Robert Peters, Morality in Media at 1, 2 (Aug. 14, 2002) [hereinafter MIM]; Comment by Nancy Ledeboer, Las Vegas-Clark County Library District at 1, 2 (Aug. 21, 2002) [hereinafter Ledeboer]; Comment by American Center for Law and Justice at 3 (Aug. 26, 2002) [hereinafter ACLJ]; Comment by Nancy Willard at 7 (Aug. 27, 2002) [hereinafter Willard].

[37] Comment by Shelly Murray at 1 (Aug. 1, 2002); Bosley, *supra* note 36, at 1.

block with the option to "unlock" those sites at a later time.[38] One public library described filters as "easy to use," giving students "access to most sites they need in school."[39] The library also reported few, if any, problems associated with filtered Internet use.[40]

NTIA also received comments that referenced the results of 26 independent laboratory tests on filters conducted between 1995 and 2001 by ten professional testing laboratories.[41] (See Appendix III) The labs conducted 108 individual product tests examining filtering software. The test results grouped products into three categories: "found filters effective," "found filters of mixed effectiveness," and "found filters ineffective." Nineteen of the twenty-six product tests found filters effective, four product tests found filters of mixed effectiveness, and three product tests found filters ineffective. Based on these results, the commenters that drew NTIA's attention to this study concluded that filtering is an effective method of protecting children from inappropriate material.[42]

Where filtering fell short of being effective, the situation usually involved either overblocking or underblocking of material. Numerous commenters discussed the effect of overblocking and underblocking of online content as it relates to the needs of educational institutions.[43] The United States District Court for the Eastern District of Pennsylvania defined overblocking as, "the blocking of content that does not meet the category definitions established by CIPA or by the filtering software companies," and underblocking as "leaving off of a control list a URL that contains content that would meet the category definitions defined by CIPA or the filtering software companies."[44]

---

[38] Comment by Gina Montgomery at 1 (June 4, 2002).

[39] Bosley, *supra* note 36, at 1.

[40] *Id.*

[41] Comment by N2H2 at 13 (Aug. 27, 2002) [hereinafter N2H2]; ACLJ, *supra* note 36, at 3. The results from these tests have been compiled into the report, "The Facts on Filters," authored by David Burt. The labs conducting these tests include: ZD Net Labs, Consumer Reports Labs, Camden Associates, IW Labs, eWeek Labs, the PC World Test Center, the Info World Test Center, MacWorld Labs, Network World Test Alliance, and Real-World Labs.

[42] ACLJ, *supra* note 36, at 3.

[43] NTIA's Request for Comment did not seek comments of the constitutionality of the CIPA statute or its provisions. Several commenters directed NTIA to the National Research Council study, *Youth, Pornography, and the Internet*, released in May 2002. Comment by Richard Cate, State Education Department, University of the State of New York at 2 (Aug. 22, 2002) [hereinafter Cate]; CDT, *supra* note 36, at 3,4; Comment by Parry Aftab, WiredSafety.org at 2 (July 15, 2002) [hereinafter Aftab]; Comment by Anita Carter, Palo Alto Unified School District at 1 (August 10, 2002); Comment by American Civil Liberties Union and Electronic Privacy Information Center at 1-2 (Aug. 27, 2002) [hereinafter ACLU]. Among other things, the report studied the many existing ways to block content with technology. The section analyzing filters explains that filters are subject to two kinds of inevitable errors: overblocking and underblocking. National Research Council, *supra* note 8, at 51, 58.

[44] American Library Association v. United States, 201 F. Supp.2d 401, 431-432 (E.D. Pa. 2002).

One concern resulting from overblocking is the restricted ability of users to view appropriate content and legitimate online research.[45] Comments from the education community acknowledged that despite training and education, technology still fails to meet the needs of educators by missing inappropriate sites, or by depriving students and teachers of access to legitimate information. Two commenters expressed particular concern with the latter situation.[46] A study by the Pew Internet and American Life Project recently found that: "[w]hile many students recognize the need to shelter teenagers from inappropriate material and adult-oriented commercial ads, they complain that blocking and filtering software often raises barriers to students' legitimate educational use of the Internet. Most of our students feel that filtering software blocks important information, and many feel discouraged from using the Internet by the difficulties they face in accessing educational material." [47]

Other comments referred to the United States District Court for the Eastern District of Pennsylvania's May 24, 2002 decision declaring CIPA Sections 1712 and Section 1721 facially invalid under the First Amendment.[48] A three-judge panel convened an eight-day trial to decide the issues related to the effectiveness of currently available technology protection measures.[49] The commenters directed NTIA's attention to the court's discussion of the difficulties with the Internet's structural composition that impinge upon the filtering software's ability to block content effectively.[50]

The court described the Internet as a decentralized, interconnected network with millions of web pages linked to thousands of additional web pages to create the "publicly indexable web." [51] These links enable search engines to sort and index material by following links from one web page to another.[52] Accordingly, search engines often fail to categorize isolated web pages not connected by these links.[53] Witness testimony estimated that fifty percent of the Internet

---

[45] CDT, *supra* note 36, at 4.

[46] Comment by National Education Association at 4 (Aug. 27, 2002) [hereinafter NEA]; International Society for Technology in Education at 4 (Aug. 27, 2002) [hereinafter ISTE].

[47] The Pew Internet and American Life Project, *The Digital Disconnect: The Widening Gap Between Internet-Savvy Students and their Schools* (August 14, 2002), *available at* http://www.pewinternet.org/reports/toc.asp?Report=67.

[48] American Library Association v. United States, 201 F. Supp.2d 401 (E.D. Pa. 2002).

[49] *Id.*

[50] CDT, *supra* note 36, at 3; Comment by Consortium for School Networking at 4 (Aug. 16, 2002) [hereinafter COSN]; Comment by American Library Association at 2 (Aug. 26, 2002) [hereinafter ALA]; ACLU, *supra* note 43, at 1-2.

[51] American Library Association v. United States, 201 F. Supp.2d at 418.

[52] *Id.*

[53] *Id.*

currently remains incapable of being indexed, thereby further invalidating the effectiveness of filtering technologies.[54]

The court heard testimony from three leading filtering companies who explained the methods used to filter content.[55] Typically, filtering software products separate appropriate and inappropriate content by compiling category lists such as: adult/sexually explicit, arts, alcohol, business, chat, dating, education, entertainment, hate speech, health, illegal, news, religion, and violence.[56] Users determine which content to block by selecting from pre-determined category lists.[57]

Additional testimony was to the effect that the filtering technologies are incapable of effectively blocking the majority of content defined by CIPA without also blocking a substantial amount of protected speech.[58] As indicated by government witnesses, every filtering software product demonstrated excluded between 6 percent and 15 percent of protected speech.[59] The court evaluated why filtering software overblocked or underblocked material and concluded that: filtering companies focus on reviewing fresh content or newly posted web addresses and spend little time on reviewing the accuracy of websites previously categorized; inconsistencies exist between filtering definitions for pornography and CIPA's legal definitions of obscenity, child pornography, or content harmful to minors; community standards vary with regard to categorizing content; and the available technology is generally unable to meet CIPA's requirement that filters block visual depictions, but not text.[60]

Based on the comments, existing technology protection measures are helping to meet the concerns of educational institutions to protect children from inappropriate materials they may encounter while using the Internet. The occurrence of overblocking and underblocking, however, has resulted in some dissatisfaction and frustration by users with the existing technology protection measures.

B.   Accessing Online Educational Materials with a Minimum Level of Relevant Content Being Blocked.

While existing technology protection measures, such as filtering software, are able to block much of which is deemed inappropriate material for children, the technology measures

---

[54] Id.

[55] Id. at 436-437.

[56] Id. at 442-443.

[57] Id.

[58] Id. at 446-448.

[59] Id. at 442.

[60] Id. at 446-448.

also sometimes block online educational content sought by teachers. Commenters from both individual schools and associations representing schools discussed the difficulties that educators experience when planning lessons based on online content. The Consortium for School Networking (COSN) polled their members and found that filtering and blocking technologies often block lessons planned by teachers from home, including educational websites.[61] For example, this experience caused frustration for a program in Missouri that furnishes teachers with laptops for the specific purpose of preparing lessons at home. The technology in these schools often blocks access to web sites pre-selected by teachers. Teachers in these schools usually discover the blocked web sites during a lesson, forcing them to react quickly and find new, suitable content.

One response to this situation is the COSN's June 2001 report, "Safeguarding the Wired Schoolhouse," which provides guidance to educators using the Internet to supplement their lessons with educational content and resources that evaluate web sites, search strategies, search engines, and web lessons.[62] Two examples provided in the report include the Montgomery County Public Schools' and the Washington Library Media Association's development of websites about information literacy and the creation of web lessons.[63]

Congress included several "disabling provisions" within CIPA allowing administrators to disable technology for certain *bona fide* research or other lawful purposes.[64] Although some claim that Congress intended these provisions to cure the overblocking tendencies of technology protection measures,[65] some commenters expressed concern that the provisions affect differently those recipients receiving E-rate funds and those receiving Department of Education funds.[66] For example, the recipients of Department of Education funds may "disable for certain use"[67] and recipients of E-rate funds may "disable during adult use."[68] The comments further

---

[61] COSN, *supra* note 50, at 14, 15.

[62] The Consortium for School Networking, *Safeguarding the Wired Schoolhouse* (June 2001) at 11.

[63] *Id.* at 27.

[64] CIPA Section 1711(a)(3) (codified at 20 U.S.C. § 6777(c)(2003)); CIPA Section 1712(a)(3) (codified at 20 U.S.C. § 9134(b)(2003)); CIPA Section 1721(a) (codified at 47 U.S.C. 254(h)(5)(D)(2003)); CIPA Section 1721(b) (codified at 47 U.S.C. 254(h)(6)(D)(2003)).

[65] American Library Association v. United States, 201 F. Supp.2d 401, 484-486 (E.D. Pa. 2002).

[66] ISTE, *supra* note 46, at 9; NEA, *supra* note 46, at 8; COSN, *supra* note 50, at 10, 11.

[67] Disabling During Certain Use, CIPA Section 1711(a)(3) (codified at 20 U.S.C. § 6777(c)(2003)) (stating that an administrator, supervisor, or person authorized by the responsible authority under paragraph (1) may disable the technology protection measure concerned to enable access for *bona fide* research or other lawful purposes); CIPA Section 1712(a)(3) (codified at 20 U.S.C. § 9134(b)(2003)) (stating that an administrator, supervisor, or other authority may disable a technology protection measure under paragraph (1) to enable access for bona fide or other lawful purposes).

[68] Disabling During Adult Use, CIPA Section 1721(a) (codified at 47 U.S.C. 254(h)(5)(D)(2003)) (stating that an administrator, supervisor, or other person authorized by the certifying authority under subparagraph (A)(i) may

explained that "disabling for certain use" permits administrators to supersede technology for both adults and students, whereas "disabling during adult use," limits a school's flexibility to supersede technology.[69] Some schools noted that by creating different standards based on the source of federal funds, these provisions generate confusion and reluctance within educational communities about using disabling technology to accommodate override requests for fear of breaching CIPA.[70] Some commenters perceived the override provision as failing to cure the overblocking concerns when educators or students desire immediate access to educationally-related material.[71]

Based on the comments, some educators are having difficulties with existing technology protection measures in meeting their need to be able to access online educational materials with a minimum level of relevant content being blocked. The disabling provisions of CIPA do not appear to be a satisfactory answer for some educators.

C.   Deciding on the Local Level How Best to Protect Children from Internet Dangers.

Several commenters stated that CIPA's provisions requiring educational institutions to install technology protection measures on computers removes local decision making from educators.[72] Comments from associations representing schools explained that schools often adopt locally-based Internet solutions reflecting the unique circumstances of the community, such as: faculty and staff familiarity with technology; level of patron and parental involvement; values of the community; funding resources; size of the community and educational institution; degree of supervision; education philosophy; and political will of library and school board members.[73] Further, schools prefer making decisions locally to reflect local resources (financial and human), values, and community concerns.[74]

Commenters also tended to disagree regarding the access to selection criteria developed by software companies for filtering products. For example, educators argue that, without an understanding of how technology companies select blocking criteria, educators possibly subject

---

disable the technology protection measure concerned, during use by an adult, to enable access for bona fide research or other lawful purpose); CIPA Section 1721(b) (codified at 47 U.S.C. 254(h)(6)(D)(2003)) (stating that an administrator, supervisor, or other person authorized by the certifying authority under subparagraph (A)(i) may disable the technology protection measure concerned, during use by an adult, to enable access for *bona fide* research or other lawful purpose).

[69] ISTE, *supra* note 46, at 11.

[70] COSN, *supra* note 50, at 15.

[71] Willard, *supra* note 36, at 2; ACLU, *supra* note 43, at 1, 2; CDT, *supra* note 36, at 2.

[72] ISTE, *supra* note 46, at 5; NEA, *supra* note 46, at 2.

[73] *Id.*

[74] NEA, *supra* note 46, at 2.

themselves to non-educational standards and the ideas and policies of outside parties.[75] Yet, according to the comments submitted by a technology developer of blocking and filtering software, the company provides extensive information to users and publishes details about the categories of sites it blocks.[76] Several vendors' comments discussed their products' ability to allow users to type in a web address to learn more about a particular site's blocking category.[77] Additionally, one vendor discussed its efforts to seek user feedback and to respond promptly to consumer requests to add, delete, or change a blocked web site.[78] To that end, the company received over 60,000 requests between January 1, 2002 and August 15, 2002, and reviewed each request within two days.[79] Of these requests, twenty percent resulted in an addition, deletion or change.[80]

On the other hand, two commenters noted that many technology companies choose not to release their blocked lists for a variety of reasons including: the list's proprietary nature and source code; the risk of abuse by competitors; the expense associated with a carefully created database; the harmful effect to children; the diminished value of a published list; and the general privacy policy of the company.[81] In addition, the National Education Association's comments stated that, generally, category descriptions vary in scope, detail, and helpfulness.[82] One advocacy group claimed that the employees of filtering companies may apply their own subjective judgments or reflect the manufacturers' social and political views when reviewing content web sites.[83]

In addition to preferring that technology companies release their lists of blocked sites, educational institutions questioned the process filtering companies use to develop and define blocking criteria. The American Library Association expressed uneasiness with selecting technology tools to accommodate the wide-ranging values of their patrons when most libraries feel uncertainty about the blocking decisions made by companies.[84] The Center for Democracy and Technology agreed that technology users enjoy little input into blocking decisions, noting

---

[75] Comment by Dr. Patrick Greene, Florida Gulf Coast University at 1 (Aug. 8, 2002) [hereinafter Greene]; Willard, *supra* note 36, at 1.

[76] N2H2, *supra* note 41, at 7.

[77] *Id.*; Comment by Nicole Toomey Davis, DoBox at 1 (July 25, 2002) [hereinafter DoBox].

[78] N2H2, *supra* note 41, at 8.

[79] *Id.* at 12.

[80] *Id.*

[81] NEA, *supra* note 46, at 5; N2H2, *supra* note 41, at 8.

[82] NEA, *supra* note 46, at 5.

[83] Comment by Free Expression Policy Project at 2 (Aug. 26, 2002) [hereinafter FEPP].

[84] ALA, *supra* note 50, at 1.

that, "in designing filtering tools, companies seek to meet the needs of diverse consumer groups and thus intentionally choose to block sites that may be undesirable or offensive to a particular audience or targeted consumer group but deemed appropriate by another."[85]

Many commenters cited to the U.S. District Court decision to highlight the desire of educational institutions to make decisions locally, and the need to understand categories pre-selected by filtering companies. Additionally, commenters discussed that the blocking categories defined by filtering companies rarely correspond with CIPA's definition and these categories cannot be customized to comply with CIPA.[86]

The comments underscored in a number of ways the belief by some educational institutions that existing technology measures fell short of meeting their need to decide locally how to protect the children in their community from Internet dangers.

D.   Understanding How to Fully Utilize Internet Protection Technology Measures.

The comments indicated that educators need training to fully understand how to use the technology protection measures in order to accommodate *bona fide* and other lawful research, as well as to meet other needs of their specific environment. Several comments noted the difficulty of adjusting a technology tool to override a blocked web site.[87] Many commenters acknowledged that overblocking of helpful educational material occurs with many filtering products and, consequently, teachers need training on how to disable filtering software for minors conducting educational searches or other legitimate research.[88]

The commenters also noted instances where educators experienced delays with an override.[89] The Consortium of School Networking (COSN) asked their members to report their experience with override requests. They found that the time it took to request an override and receive a response ranged from less than five minutes to as long as one week.[90] Some institutions lacked an override policy altogether.[91] One association's comments summarized the

---

[85] CDT, *supra* note 36, at 4.

[86] ACLU, *supra* note 43, at 6; FEPP, *supra* note 83, at 2; COSN, *supra* note 50, at 4.

[87] Willard, *supra* note 36, at 6; NEA, *supra* note 46, at 7.

[88] NEA, supra note 46, at 4; ISTE, *supra* note 46, at 4.

[89] Willard, *supra* note 36, at 3. According to Willard, when teachers direct students to use home computers, this practice impedes the education of students without home computers. Willard further argues that this situation results in an ineffective use of the expensive computer technology that has been installed in schools.

[90] COSN, *supra* note 50, at 15.

[91] *Id.*

end result of these issues as extremely frustrating for teachers who lack training on how to disable filtering technology.[92]

NTIA also received a variety of responses discussing educators' experience with adjusting technology protection measures to accommodate all age groups and grades. The comments indicate the need for training educators on how to adjust technology protection measures to accommodate different age groups. One commenter stated that its filtering technology does not adjust blocking content based on the age of the child.[93] Yet, many technology products offer users the ability to customize.[94] One technology vendor provided NTIA with an example of its product's web site customization feature.[95] Specifically, the product gives the user the ability to add sites to a block list.[96] Another commenter described a software program that accommodates six age groups: unfiltered access-adults; teen access-15 to 17; pre-teen-12 to 14; kid-8 to 11; child-7 & under.[97] While many products exist that adjust to different ages, some commenters disagreed with the effectiveness or ease of adjusting the technology to accommodate various ages or grades.[98] One commenter noted that relying on age specific categories works well for younger children, but varying maturity levels makes it more difficult to cluster older children by age and rely upon the categories pre-selected by technology vendors.[99]

Based on the comments, existing technology protection measures are capable of meeting a number of the needs of educational institutions. However, some educators are unaware of the capabilities of these measures or lack the knowledge about how to use many features of the technology protection tools.

E.   Considering a Variety of Technical, Educational, and Economic Factors When Selecting Technology Protection Measures.

Commenters listed several factors that educational institutions take into account prior to selecting technology. Most commenters cited cost as the primary factor. One commenter mentioned that when institutions consider cost, they often choose cheaper and less sophisticated

---

[92] *Id.*

[93] Ledeboer, *supra* note 36, at 2.

[94] DoBox, *supra* note 77, at 3, 5; N2H2, *supra* note 41, at 31; Comment by Kidsnet at 3 (Aug. 27, 2003) [hereinafter Kidsnet].

[95] DoBox, *supra* note 77, at 12.

[96] *Id.* at 3.

[97] ACLJ, *supra* note 36, at 4.

[98] Cate, *supra* note 43, at 3; ISTE, *supra* note 46, at 2.

[99] ISTE, *supra* note 46, at 2; Willard, *supra* note 36, at 7.

products.[100] Schools and libraries also noted that they obtain very little extra funding to pay for Internet protection measures.[101] The E-Rate program, which gives schools and libraries discounts on telephone service, Internet access, and internal connections, does not cover technology protection measures, such as filtering and blocking software.[102] In addition to cost, comments from educational associations listed maintenance, effectiveness, ability to customize, network impact, and upgrades as important factors considered when selecting technology protection measures.[103] In sum, the commenters noted that educational institutions consider a variety of economic, technical, and educational factors when selecting technology protection measures.

F. Adopting an Internet Safety Strategy that Includes Technology, Human Monitoring, and Education.

Commenters responding to NTIA's Request for Comment described their experience with the use of technology protection measures within educational institutions. Many educational institutions discussed their use of filtering and blocking technology to protect children from inappropriate content. Others explained their use of a combination of technology and non-technical protection strategies, such as human monitoring or Internet safety policies, to achieve this goal.

Interestingly, the comments revealed that the measures adopted by educational institutions depend in part on their interpretation of CIPA. One commenter noted that educational institutions trying to comply with CIPA interpret the language "technology protection measures" as a requirement to install only filtering software, and often do not explore other technical remedies.[104] This commenter also stated that many educational institutions interpret CIPA's "technology protection measure" language as limited to "commercial, proprietary-protected filtering software."[105] A trade association noted that this narrow

---

[100] ISTE, *supra* note 46, at 9.

[101] Previously, schools relied on a grant established in 1996 called the Technology Challenge Fund. The Fund subsidized additional technology costs for schools not covered by the E-rate. Congress had allotted $200 million to the fund for the U.S. Department of Education to administer, but the fund expired on September 30, 2002.

[102] The Federal Communications Commission, Universal Service for Schools and Libraries, *available at* http://www.fcc.gov/wcb/universal_service/schoolsandlibs html. The Universal Service Administrative Company (USAC) administers the Schools and Libraries program, also called the E-rate program. According to USAC, approximately 82 percent of public schools and 10 percent of private schools received E-rate funding in the Fiscal Year (FY) 2000 funding cycle (July 1, 2000 through June 30, 2001) (using 1997 data base as denominator). Public libraries also rely heavily on E-rate funding--57 percent of main public libraries received E-rate funding in FY 2000. Successful applicants receive discounts ranging from 20 percent to 90 percent, depending upon the household income level of students and whether the school or library is located in a rural or urban area. The program is intended to assist local and state programs connecting schools and libraries to the Internet.

[103] COSN, *supra* note 50, at 11; NEA, *supra* note 46, at 5; ISTE, *supra* note 46, at 9.

[104] Willard, *supra* note 36, at 6.

[105] *Id.*

interpretation of CIPA's technology protection measure requirement may inhibit schools and libraries from adopting more comprehensive solutions that encompass both technology and education.[106] Some commenters did discuss other technology measures, such as monitoring software,[107] but there were no comments from educational institutions regarding their experience as users of monitoring software.

The Federal Communications Commission's (FCC) rules interpret CIPA as encouraging educational institutions to adopt both technological and non-technological measures to protect children online.[108] FCC regulations require schools and libraries to certify that they have adopted:

- An Internet safety policy that blocks and filters certain visual depictions for both minors and adults;
- An Internet safety policy that includes monitoring;
- An Internet safety policy that addresses: access to inappropriate material; email, chat, and other forms of electronic communications; hacking; disclosure of a minor's personal information; and measures restricting material that is harmful to minors.[109]

A report released in September 2002 by the U.S. Department of Education's National Center for Educational Statistics supports the conclusion that educational institutions rely on a combination approach to shield children from inappropriate online content. The report documents that, in 2001, 96 percent of public schools used a variety of technologies or policies to protect children from inappropriate content. Of these schools, 91 percent relied on teacher or staff monitoring; 87 percent installed blocking or filtering software; 80 percent required parents to sign a written contract; 75 percent required students to sign a written contract; 44 percent adopted an honor code; and 26 percent confined school access to an intranet.[110]

Notwithstanding some commenters' interpretation of CIPA, the majority of comments indicated that most educational institutions prefer a combination of technology and education to ensure a safe online environment.[111] Members of the International Society of Technology in Education (ISTE) adopted numerous methods to ensure that students had a safe, educational, and

---

[106] Comment by Mid Atlantic Regional Technology in Education Consortium (MAR*TEC) at 1 (Aug. 27, 2002) [hereinafter MAR*TEC].

[107] Willard, *supra* note 36, at 7; Comment by Vericept at 1 (Aug. 27, 2002) [hereinafter Vericept].

[108] Federal-State Joint Board on Universal Service, CC Docket No. 96-45, Report and Order, FCC 01-120 (April 5, 2001).

[109] *Id.* at 3, 4.

[110] National Center for Education Statistics, *supra* note 4, at 10.

[111] *See, e.g.,* MAR*TEC, *supra* note 106, at 1.

age appropriate experience online, including acceptable use policies, software technologies, teacher monitoring and supervision, and student education programs.[112] A trade association representing schools stated that most educational institutions adopt diverse Internet protection solutions that correspond with the culture and resources of their community.[113]

Several commenters indicated a preference for non-technological solutions or a need to supplement technology with non-technical measures to create a safe online environment. For example, the State Education Department of the University of the State of New York relies on broadly written acceptable use policies as their protection method of choice. It views technology-based solutions as geared toward content issues only, leaving the other challenges associated with public Internet access unaddressed. Thus, it adopted written policies to manage a wide-range of additional specific behaviors, such as patron access, noise levels, and computer tampering.[114]

A school in Albuquerque, New Mexico, took a different approach. As an individual serving as a volunteer school technology coordinator explained, the school adopted student monitoring and pre-selected sites over filtering technology, not only because of the unreliability of technology and the cost, but also because of an inadequate budget to train staff.[115] This commenter concludes that the creation of "yes" lists, or pre-selected child-appropriate content, serves to keep children protected from harmful content.[116]

Some libraries are also emphasizing a non-technical approach to safeguarding children from harmful content. The Board of the Evanston Public Library in Illinois implemented a library use policy instead of filtering software for its computers. The policy encourages parents to accompany their children and supervise their Internet access. Additionally, librarians configure children's computers for "focused Internet access," directing kids to pre-select age-appropriate websites.[117] The Charles M. Bailey Public Library in Winthrop, Maine utilizes a combination of bookmarks, web design, parental involvement, and technology education classes for children to create a safe online environment.[118] The Las Vegas Clark County Library District (LVCCLD) uses an approach giving patrons numerous options to protect themselves online. The

---

[112] ISTE, *supra* note 46, at 5.

[113] COSN, *supra* note 50, at 11.

[114] Cate, *supra* note 43, at 1.

[115] Comment by David Duggan at 1, 3 (Aug. 26, 2002) [hereinafter Duggan].

[116] *Id.* at 1.

[117] Comment by Janice Bojda, Evanston Public Library at 1 (Aug. 27, 2002) [hereinafter Bojda] (stating that libraries make web page selection choices using the same standards as they do to select materials in their hard copy selection).

[118] Ranney, *supra* note 36, at 1.

library prefers an "empowerment" approach offering patrons the choice to control their Internet access level with various educational and informational methods.[119]

Based on the comments, existing technology protection measures are capable of meeting the technology component of an approach that includes both technology and non-technical protection strategies.

In sum, NTIA gleaned six distinct needs within educational institutions: (1) balancing the importance of allowing children to use the Internet with the importance of protecting children from inappropriate material; (2) accessing online educational materials with a minimum level of relevant content being blocked; (3) deciding locally how best to protect children from Internet dangers; (4) understanding how to fully utilize Internet protection technology measures; (5) considering a variety of technical, educational, and economic factors when selecting technology protection measures; and (6) adopting an Internet safety strategy that includes technology, human monitoring, and education. As articulated in the comments, existing technology protection measures, by themselves, are meeting most, but not all, of these needs. Below we discuss ways to foster the development of measures that would more fully meet these needs of educational institutions.

III. Fostering the Development of Measures that Meet the Needs of Educational Institutions

In the comments, NTIA found that educational institutions experienced frustration with the marketplace for not developing new and advanced technology protection measures. NTIA asked commenters to discuss the development of new technology features that would better meet the needs of educational institutions. NTIA received a variety of responses indicating that the following technology features would best assist educational institutions today.

- Technology that scans a website's content, rather than relying on key words;[120]
- Customer access to lists of blocked sites by subject area;[121]
- Individual logins to allow flexibility in grades kindergarten through 12 or child/adult settings;[122]
- Ability of a system administrator or local technician to edit or override blocked sites in real time;[123] and
- Image recognition technology.[124]

---

[119] Ledeboer, *supra* note 36, at 4.

[120] Cate, *supra* note 43, at 2.

[121] *Id.* at 3.

[122] COSN, *supra* note 50, at 15.

[123] ISTE, *supra* note 46, at 9.

Comments from four technology vendors explained how their technology blocks categorized content, and described features associated with their product. [125] The vendors offer many of the features desired by the education community. For example:

- DoBox described its technology as able to manage all facets of Internet access, including Web, email, chat/instant messaging, applications/games, and peer to peer systems. Its product allows local customization by user and by group, and allows authorized individuals to add immediately sites to be blocked or permit sites for permanent or temporary access.[126]

- Kidsnet described its product, EducationNet, as providing educators with three levels of protection: (1) relying on 100 percent human review of all web site content; (2) basing content review on transparent and adaptable criteria; and (3) adapting categories to fit various ages or levels and different needs of institutions.[127]

- N2H2 relies on a confidential and proprietary database of 42 categories, giving users the choice of any or all of these categories. N2H2 updates the database and creates a new version daily. N2H2 follows four steps to categorize sites: (1) flag URLs for categorization; (2) match and flag URL for review; (3) examine and categorize; and (4) reexamine URLs in database. N2H2 also publicly releases details, descriptions, and criteria of the 42 content categories on their website.[128]

- The Vericept Corporation, formally known as E-sniff, combines URL filtering with "comprehensive content monitoring" for all forms of Internet access. Vericept described "comprehensive content monitoring" as tools that track all inappropriate content flowing through the network. Users determine "inappropriate" content based upon reports generated from network traffic.[129]

Based on the four descriptions, these existing products offer features similar to those requested by educational institutions.

---

[124] ACLU, *supra* note 43, at 4 (stating that CIPA requires technology protection measures to block images, yet image recognition technology is immature).

[125] NTIA summarization of the four vendor comments should not be construed as an endorsement of any product.

[126] DoBox, *supra* note 77, at 1.

[127] Kidsnet, *supra* note 94, at 1.

[128] N2H2, *supra* note 41, at 4.

[129] Vericept, *supra* note 107, at 1.

Through independent research, NTIA also found that more companies are increasingly entering the market for Internet content protection technology. Some analysts predict that the growth of the networking and protection market can be attributed to increased Internet access, the exponential growth of web pages, and the increasing desire of families, schools, and libraries to protect children from inappropriate content and interactions on the Internet.[130] Some analysts predict that the market for these products will rise to over $600 million by 2004 at a rate of nearly 50 percent per year.[131]

The more-established Internet content filtering companies appear to be increasing the amount of money that they put into their research and development divisions.[132] Numerous venture capital firms invest in these Internet-safety technology companies as well, both within the United States and abroad.[133] In addition to U.S.-made Internet content filters, international companies are developing filtering software. Currently, over fifty companies exist that provide this technology.[134] NTIA found that while a substantial number of technology companies exist that invest in the research and development of technology protection measures, educational institutions are either unaware of the diverse array of products available to meet their needs or lack the training to fully utilize the products.

Some commenters claim that CIPA locked in filtering and blocking technology as the "technology protection measure" of choice, thereby stifling potential innovation of technology protection measures.[135] According to several commenters, little incentive exists for the markets to develop more flexible technology products to meet the needs of educational institutions if investors or venture capitalists perceive the education community as demanding only one type of technology.[136] The Consortium for School Networking writes that CIPA "forced all of the companies competing in the market to define their product in terms of which best complies with CIPA, rather than how they may serve the needs of different kinds of school districts." [137]

While some commenters encouraged technology vendors to develop new protection products to meet educators' needs, others believed that the focus of attention should not be on

---

[130] *Content Filtering of the Web Gains Foothold in Corporate Market*, The Wall Street Journal Europe, April 11, 2001.

[131] *Id.*

[132] IPO.COM at http://www.IPO.com/ipoinfo/search.asp?p=IPO&srange=1900&pstart=1/1/1998 (last viewed March 2003. Site no longer available).

[133] *Id.*

[134] PEP: Resources for Parents, Educators, and Publishers, *Guide to Parental Controls/Internet Safety Products*, at http://www.microweb.com/pepsite/Software/filters.html.

[135] ISTE, *supra* note 46, at 7.

[136] *Id.*; Willard, *supra* note 36, at 6; COSN, *supra* note 50, at 12.

[137] COSN, *supra* note 50, at 12; Willard, *supra* note 36, at 6; DoBox, *supra* note 77, at 1.

new technologies.[138] Rather, they believe that the focus of attention should be on the development and implementation of a comprehensive education and supervision approach to protect children by preparing them to make safe and responsible choices.[139]

A.   NTIA Recommendations

Section 1703(a)(2) of CIPA invited NTIA to make any recommendations to Congress on how to foster the development of measures that meet the needs of educational institutions.[140] Based on the comments, NTIA has identified two recommendations: (1) vendors should offer training services to educational institutions so the institutions can understand and use fully the capabilities of technology protection measures; and (2) Congress should amend CIPA's language to clarify the term "technology protection measures."

1.   Recommendation #1: Training

The majority of comments from educational institutions noted that some educators often lack the training necessary to use fully the available technology tools. For example, although CIPA includes several provisions giving adults the authority to override technology for certain *bona fide* or other legitimate research,[141] some educators often do not know how to disable the technology. Commenters also indicated their desire that software perform specific tasks, such as scanning content rather than relying on key words; listing blocked sites by subject area; allowing individual log-ins to accommodate varying ages; and allowing editing and overriding of blocked sites in real time.[142] NTIA identified a disconnect between the specific needs listed by educational entities and the current capabilities of available technology. NTIA found that, while commenters discussed the desire for certain technological capabilities, the vendors' comments explained that their technology already performs many of these tasks.

NTIA recognizes that, as educational institutions become familiar with using technology protection measures, the need for training may decrease. Until that time, however, NTIA agrees with commenters who expressed the importance of training as part of the solution to protect children from illicit online content. NTIA suggests that as part of promotional efforts to advertise products or as part of the initial orientation to their products, technology vendors should train and educate teachers, administrative personnel, librarians, and other educational personnel on the specific features of their product.

2.   Recommendation #2: Legislative Language

---

[138] Willard, *supra* note 36, at 6.

[139] *Id.*

[140] CIPA Section 1703(a)(2), Pub. L. No. 106-554 (2000).

[141] CIPA, *supra* note 64.

[142] Cate, *supra* note 43, at 2; COSN, *supra* note 50, at 15; ISTE, *supra* note 46, at 9.

Commenters discussed the difficulty that some educational institutions have interpreting CIPA's "technology protection measure" language. Some commenters claim that many educational institutions default to "filtering" technology only, without researching other types of technology protection options. As a result, many believe that this reliance on mostly filtering products stifles the marketplace and serves as a disincentive for technology companies to invest in the research and development of newer and more sophisticated products. Moreover, as set forth above, filtering and blocking software has not been able to overcome problems of overblocking, inability to generate an updated index for the Internet, and lack of correspondence to statutory definitions and categories. Yet, other technology tools can or have the potential to address better the needs of educational institutions. Thus, NTIA recommends that Congress change the current legislation to clarify that the term "technology protection measure" encompasses not only filtering and blocking software, but also other current and future technology tools. Specifically, Section 1703(3) of CIPA currently reads as follows:

Technology Protection Measure – The term "technology protection measure" means a specific technology that blocks or filters Internet access to visual depictions that are -- (a) obscene, as that term is defined in section 1460 of title 18, United States Code; (b) child pornography, as that term is defined in section 2256 of title 18, United States Code; or (c) harmful to minors.

NTIA recommends replacing the above language with the following:

Technology Protection Measures – The term "technology protection measure" means a specific technology that *prevents* Internet access to visual depictions that are -- (a) obscene, as that term is defined in section 1460 of title 18, United States Code; (b) child pornography, as that term is defined in section 2256 of title 18, United States Code; or (c) harmful to minors.

NTIA believes this expanded definition using the word "prevents" will encourage educational institutions to utilize technology, in addition to blocking and filtering software, that may better meet their needs as outlined above. A wider selection of products should give local decision makers more options to find the products that best meet their community's needs.

Alternatively to amending CIPA, NTIA recommends that the FCC and the U.S. Department of Education (DOE) provide further guidance to recipients of E-rate or DOE funds on the meaning of technology protection measures.

IV. The Development and Effectiveness of Internet Safety Policies

NTIA found that educational institutions have engaged in discussions with their respective communities to create acceptable Internet safety policies.[143] (See Appendix IV for

---

[143] ISTE, *supra* note 46, at 5; Comment by Karen Gillespie, Grayson County Public Library at 1 (Aug. 8, 2002); Comment by Janice Friesen, eMINTS at 2 (Aug. 9, 2002) [hereinafter eMINTS]; Ranney, *supra* note 36, at 1;

examples.) Educational institutions tend to incorporate the values and needs of their community into their policy and, as a result, experience positive feedback about their policy's success as part of the solution to protect children online.[144] Most of the commenters expressed a great deal of satisfaction with the evolution and use of safety policies and praised CIPA for giving educational institutions the autonomy to develop their own policies.[145] The Consortium for School Networking (COSN) expressed appreciation that CIPA allowed schools to draft policies reflecting the needs of the community and school environment.[146] The State Education Department of the University of the State of New York credits its safety policies as the most effective strategy employed to keep patrons in conformance with library rules.[147] The policy's success begins with staff-wide understanding of the policy's content, followed by consistent application, on-going review, and community involvement.[148]

Several public libraries post Internet safety policies that appear whenever a patron logs onto a public computer.[149] In these instances, Internet access requires patrons to click an acceptance explaining his or her agreement and asks the individual to abide by the terms of the policy. The policy states that patrons may access constitutionally- protected online material, and that patrons may not use the Internet in an inappropriate manner for a public area. The policy also lists specific, prohibited behaviors, such as accessing obscene material, accessing materials harmful to minors, or engaging in offensive, intimidating, or hostile behavior. In the two years since implementing the policy, these librarians indicate that they have witnessed only a few instances of inappropriate patron behavior, and attribute their Internet safety policy with contributing to a trouble-free environment and creating a safe-online experience.[150]

Educational institutions also consider Internet safety policies as an avenue to teach children about online safety skills.[151] Some suggested important safety skills may include teaching children about taking appropriate actions when harmful content appears online; teaching children to report threatening/disturbing correspondence online; or arming children with

---

Bosley, *supra* note 36, at 1; Comment by Jason Stone, East Brunswick Public Library, East Brunswick, NJ at 1 (Aug. 14, 2002) [hereinafter EBPL]; Ledeboer, *supra* note 36, at 2; Bojda, *supra* note 117, at 1.

[144] ISTE, *supra* note 46, at 5.

[145] COSN, *supra* note 50, at 16; NEA, *supra* note 46, at 2; MAR*TEC, *supra* note 106, at 1; EBPL, *supra* note 143, at 1; Ledeboer, *supra* note 36, at 1; ISTE, *supra* note 46, at 13; CDT, *supra* note 36, at 3; Cate, *supra* note 43, at 1.

[146] COSN, *supra* note 50, at 16.

[147] Cate, *supra* note 43, at 1.

[148] *Id.*

[149] EBPL, *supra* note 143, at 1; Ledeboer, *supra* note 36, at 1.

[150] Ledeboer, *supra* note 36, at 1.

[151] COSN, *supra* note 50, at 17; NEA, *supra* note 46, at 2; Aftab, *supra* note 43, at 19; ISTE, *supra* note 46, at 13; CDT, *supra* note 36, at 3.

strategies if approached by a stranger.[152]   Additionally, one commenter underscored that Internet safety policies must be reviewed regularly to guarantee that they adequately reflect the views of the community and cover the appropriate technology.[153]

NTIA found that Internet safety policies are generally effective when educational institutions customize Internet safety policies to the needs of the community. Many communities opt to keep their policies flexible to adapt to evolving technologies and the changing needs of the community.[154]

The National Research Council report studied Acceptable Use Policies, similar to the Internet safety policy.   The report defined acceptable use policies as "a set of guidelines and expectations about how individuals will conduct themselves online."[155]   Accordingly, these policies make young people responsible for their online behavior and encourage personal accountability for responsible Internet use.[156]   The report endorses effective policies as including sanctions for violations; soliciting input from parents, community members, schools, libraries, and students; and using accidental violations as opportunities to educate users about how to avoid similar situations.[157]

NTIA asked participants to discuss their experience with successful Internet safety approaches or "best practices." NTIA grouped the responses into the following categories: acceptable use policies, child media literacy, parental education and awareness, staff education and development, identification of appropriate content, and child-safe areas. A summary of successful best practices provided by the comments is detailed below:

A. Best Practices

- Acceptable Use Policies
    - *Post guidelines and consequences for Internet use:* Ensure appropriate behavior through awareness of the policy guidelines and consequences, followed by consistent enforcement of the policy. Authorize staff to terminate Internet sessions for users who fail to comply with the policy.[158]
    - *On-screen Appropriate Use Policy:* Require Internet users to agree to abide by these policies before gaining access to the Internet.

---

[152] Aftab, *supra* note 43, at 9-28.

[153] ISTE, *supra* note 46, at 13.

[154] *Id.* at 5; NEA, *supra* note 46, at 9.

[155] National Research Council, *supra* note 8, at 235.

[156] *Id.*

[157] *Id.* at 235-236.

[158] EBPL, *supra* note 143, at 1.

- o *Age/Education criteria*: Establish flexible policies that accommodate different ages and implement education settings with varying degrees of supervision.[159]

- Child Media Literacy
    - o *Internet safety courses*: Teach students about how to use the Internet safely, report bad activity, ignore and report harassment or threats, protect their privacy and personal information, and detect information that is not appropriate.[160]
    - o *Online safety videos*: Provide students, parents, and teachers with a video teaching Internet safety and successful use skills.
    - o *Internet search skills*: Teach students skills to conduct successful, safe Internet searches using keywords and search engines.[161]
    - o *Learning to evaluate online material:* Teach children to evaluate the veracity, appropriateness, and educational value of websites.[162]
    - o *Internet Drivers' Licenses:* Require students to take an Internet safety and use course, followed by a test that students must pass in order to receive the privilege of using the Internet at school.

- Parental Education and Awareness
    - o *Educate families about technology and the Internet*: Encourage parental involvement, as this often leads to safer online experiences for children.[163]
    - o *Parental supervision:* Rely not only on filters, but also on parental supervision as means of protecting children from harmful content.[164] Encourage parents to pay attention to how and when students use the Internet, and to be responsive with intervention and discipline.[165]

- Staff Education and Development
    - o *Curriculum tailored sites:* Educate teachers about how to find, bookmark, and provide for their students those web sites that complement safe teaching materials.
    - o *Teacher Training:* Train teachers to effectively use technology.

- Identification of Appropriate Content

[159] MAR*TEC, *supra* note 106, at 1.

[160] Aftab, *supra* note 43, at 19.

[161] NEA, *supra* note 46, at 3.

[162] CDT, *supra* note 36, at 7.

[163] *Id.* at 1.

[164] Bojda, *supra* note 117, at 1.

[165] Willard, *supra* note 36, at 8.

- o *Pre-approved hotlinks:* Administrators and educators pre-select safe and appropriate sites for child access.[166]
- o *Teacher lessons:* Teachers create lesson plans with laptops at home tailored to specific subject areas/curriculum. [167]
- o *Creation of pre-approved "yes" lists:* Allow access only to those sites that have been pre-approved as safe and appropriate.[168]

- Child-Safe Areas
  - o *Filtered:* Designate a specific children's computer room with filters installed on the computers. Combine filtered access with Internet education and safety.[169]
  - o *Children's monitors in public view:* Discourage use policy violations by allowing others to see the monitors.[170]
  - o *Enclosed Internet stations for adults:* Screen adult workstations from child-safe areas.

B. Lessons Learned From Internet Safety Policies

NTIA asked commenters for lessons learned from their experience with Internet safety policies. One Internet safety expert told NTIA that in order to ensure successful policies governing children's Internet use, drafters of such policies should discuss the following: guidelines/purpose, sharing networks/resources, passwords, email, privacy, copyright and plagiarism, Internet access, and safety.[171] Another group encouraged teachers and librarians to establish policies that: give educators autonomy for classroom curriculum materials; address the different ages of students and different educational settings (classroom use, library use, after school enrichment); and implement effective human and technical monitoring strategies.[172] An education trade group wrote that Internet safety policies should not be regarded as "just another form for parental signature," but rather these policies must be given special status, and the policy's principles must be fully integrated into the school curriculum.[173]

Other comments discussed the importance of incorporating clear violations and sanctions into safety policies.[174] For example, a program in Missouri encourages strong consequences of

---

[166] *Id.* at 4.

[167] eMINTS, *supra* note 143, at 1.

[168] Duggan, *supra* note 115, at 3.

[169] Ledeboer, *supra* note 36, at 2.

[170] MIM, *supra* note 36, at 1.

[171] Aftab, *supra* note 43, at 35.

[172] MAR*TEC, *supra* note 106, at 1.

[173] NEA, *supra* note 46, at 9.

[174] COSN, *supra* note 50, at 17; eMINTS, *supra* note 143, at 1.

computer misuse.[175] If a student intentionally misuses the computer, the student forfeits all computer privileges and the school informs the student's parent of the violation.[176] If a student unintentionally misuses the computer, the student must immediately turn off the computer and raise his or her hand for the teacher to handle the situation.[177] The program praised this policy as keeping violations to a minimum largely due to the policy's clarity and consistent enforcement.[178]

Commenters also noted several difficulties with employing technology without acceptable use policies to protect children. First, commenters noted that technology protection measures are not the entire answer.[179] These commenters emphasized that technology protection measures are most effective when teachers and educational institutions can customize technology and use it in connection with other strategies and tools.[180] As one commenter stated, children need to be trained to think critically and use the Internet safely. Technology cannot replace education and judgment.[181]

Second, one commenter noted that technology protection measures can give a false sense of protection.[182] This commenter stated that children should be educated to avoid improper content in the same unfiltered environments children experience in their homes, libraries, and offices. He argued that filtering provides an inauthentic atmosphere that thwarts teachers' preparing their students to deal with reality.[183]

Alternatively, another commenter argued that acceptable use policies may give a false sense of protection.[184] The commenter noted that appropriate use policies are a good protection measure, but there is an assumption that children can avoid offensive material simply by

---

[175] eMINTS, *supra* note 143, at 1.

[176] *Id.*

[177] Some commenters expressed concern with sanctions that remove computer privileges from students. Such sanctions severely disadvantage students without home computers or Internet access.

[178] eMINTS, *supra* note 143, at 1.

[179] ISTE, *supra* note 46, at 2.

[180] *Id.*

[181] *Id.*

[182] Greene, *supra* note 75, at 1.

[183] *Id.*

[184] ACLJ, *supra* note 36, at 8.

education.[185] He also contended that time limits imposed by acceptable use policies have not been found to stop the ability of children to access inappropriate material online.[186]

Another difficulty that commenters highlighted is the constraints of the school environment. They noted that the classroom setting is not always amenable to monitoring.[187] They also stated that teachers express uncertainty about their role as monitor watching children online. They noted that some teachers lack the requisite knowledge and sophistication about technology.[188]

The National Research Council report also discussed several issues relating to acceptable use policies. The Council recommended that these policies should: distinguish between adult and child use; distinguish between younger and older children; determine how to measure compliance; avoid overly broad wording and strive to list specific inappropriate behavior and material; protect against liability; and define a user's rights.[189]

The best practices and lessons learned that are set forth above provide valuable information for communities to consider as they develop and implement Internet safety policies.

V.   Conclusion

In summary, existing technology protection measures have met many of the needs of educational institutions. While the education community has had success with technology measures, however, the education community also recognizes that comprehensive child protection solutions do not rest solely with technology. Commenters emphasized that technology protection measures are most effective when teachers and educational institutions can customize technology and use it in connection with other strategies and tools. Educational institutions prefer local decision making that gives leaders the flexibility to select the appropriate technology that fits best with their unique circumstances and to consider non-economic factors that may influence technology selection decisions. Commenters also recognized the need for more training within educational institutions. Based on our evaluation of how existing technology protection measures have met the needs of educational institutions, NTIA made two recommendations: (1) additional training on the full use of technology protection measures, and (2) new legislative language that would clarify CIPA's existing "technology protection measure" language to ensure that technology protection measures include more than just blocking and filtering technology. NTIA believes this expanded definition will encourage educational

---

[185] *Id.*

[186] *Id.*

[187] MAR*TEC, *supra* note 106, at 1.

[188] *Id.*

[189] National Research Council, *supra* note 8, at 238-240.

institutions to utilize a wider range of technology that will better meet their needs. With respect to Internet safety policies, commenters reported an overwhelming satisfaction with the development and effectiveness of these policies.

NTIA also notes that the comments reveal the commitment of all interested parties – educators, academics, technology vendors, and associations – to protect children as they explore the online world. NTIA commends all the parties involved in this issue for their dedication and hard work. Our nation's children will be well served by the ongoing efforts toward effective solutions that best protect children while allowing them to reap the many benefits of the Internet.

Appendix 1. Federal Register Notice

DEPARTMENT OF COMMERCE

National Telecommunications and Information Administration

[Docket No. 020514121-2121-01]

TN 0660-XXT4

Request for Comment on the Effectiveness of Internet Protection Measures and Safety Policies

AGENCY: National Telecommunications and Information Administration, Department of Commerce.

ACTION: Notice; request for comments.

SUMMARY: The National Telecommunications and Information Administration (NTIA) invites interested parties to provide comments in response to section 1703 of the Children's Internet Protection Act (CIPA), Pub. L. No. 106-554, 114 at 2763, 2763A-336 (2000). Section 1703 directs NTIA to initiate a notice and comment proceeding to evaluate whether currently available Internet blocking or filtering technology protection measures and Internet safety policies adequately address the needs of educational institutions. The Act also directs NTIA to make recommendations to Congress on how to foster the development of technology protection measures that meet these needs.

DATES: Written comments are requested to be submitted on or before August 27, 2002.

ADDRESSES: Comments may be mailed to Salience Fortunate Chagrin, Office of Policy Analysis and Development, National Telecommunications and Information Administration, Room 4716 HCHB, 14th Street and Constitution Avenue, NW., Washington, DC 20230. Paper submissions should include a diskette in HTML, ASCII, Word, or WordPerfect format (please specify version). Diskettes should be labeled with the name and organizational affiliation of the filer, and the name of the word processing program used to create the document. In the alternative, comments may be submitted electronically to the following electronic mail address: cipa-study@ntia.doc.gov. Comments submitted via electronic mail also should be submitted in one or more of the formats specified above.

FOR FURTHER INFORMATION CONTACT: Sallianne Fortunato Schagrin, Office of Policy Analysis and Development, NTIA, telephone: (202) 482-1880; or electronic mail: sschagrin@ntia.doc.gov. Media inquiries should be directed to the Office of Public Affairs, National Telecommunications and Information Administration: telephone (202) 482-7002

SUPPLEMENTARY INFORMATION:

Growing Concern About Children's Exposure to Inappropriate Online Content

A U.S. Department of Commerce report, released earlier this year, indicates that as of September 2001 more than half of the nation's population (143 million Americans) were using the Internet. *A Nation Online: How Americans Are Expanding Their Use of the Internet*, National Telecommunications and Information Administration, U.S. Department of Commerce (Feb. 2002), available at *http://www.ntia.doc.gov/ntiahome/dn/index.html*. Children and teenagers use computers and the Internet more than any other age group. *Id.* at 1, 13. Almost go percent of children between the ages of 5 and 17 (or 48 million) now use computers. *Id.* at 1, 44. Significant numbers of children use the Internet at school or at school and home: 55 percent for 14-17 year olds; 45 percent for 10-13 year olds; and 22 percent for 5-9 year olds. *Id.* at 47. Approximately 12 percent of 10 to 17 year olds use the Internet at a library. *Id.* at 52. Noting the heightened interest regarding the possible exposure of children to unsafe or inappropriate content online, the Department of Commerce report notes that for the first time households were surveyed to determine the level of concern about their children's exposure to material over the Internet versus their concern over exposure to material on television. The results indicated that 68.3 percent of households were more concerned about the propriety of Internet content than material on television. *Id.* at 54.

Similarly, in its 2000 survey of public schools to measure Internet connectivity, the Department of Education's National Center for Education Statistics asked questions about "acceptable use policies" in schools in recognition of the concern among parents and teachers about student access to inappropriate online material. *See Internet Access in U.S. Public Schools and Classrooms: 1994-2000*, NCES 2001-071, Office of Education Research and Improvement, Department of Education (May 2001), available at *http://www.nces.ed.gov/pubs2001/internet access*.

According to the NCES survey, 98 percent of all public schools had access to the Internet by the fall of 2000. *Id.* at 1. The survey also indicated that almost all such schools had "acceptable use policies" and used various technologies or procedures (blocking or filtering software), an intranet system, student honor codes, or teacher/staff monitoring to control student access to inappropriate online material. *Id.* at 7.

Of the schools with acceptable use policies, 94 percent reported having student access to the Internet monitored by teachers or other staff; 74 percent used blocking or filtering software; 64 percent had honor codes; and 28 percent used their intranet. *Id.* Most schools (91 percent) used more than one procedure or technology as part of their policy: 15 percent used all of the procedures and technologies listed; 29 percent used blocking/ filtering software, teacher/staff monitoring, and honor codes; and 19 percent used blocking/ filtering software and teacher/staff monitoring. *Id.* at 7, 8. In addition, 95 percent of schools with an acceptable use policy used at least one of these technologies or procedures on all Internet-connected computers used by students. *Id.*

This trend appears to be reflected in the library community as well. A recent article in the Library Journal reports that of the 355 libraries responding to its Budget Report 2002, 43 percent reported filtering Internet use, up from 31 percent in 2001, and 25 percent in 2000. Norman Oder, *The New Wariness,* The Library Journal (Jan. 15, 2002) (LJ Budget Report 2002), available at *http://1ibraryjournal.reviewsnews.com/index. asp?layout=articlePrint &articleID--CA188739*. Of those libraries filtering Internet use, 96 percent reported using filters on all children's terminals. *Id.*

The E-Rate and CIPA

Section 254(h) of the Communications Act of 1934, as amended by the Telecommunications Act of 1996, provides a universal support mechanism program (commonly known as the "E-Rate program") through which eligible schools and libraries may apply for discounted telecommunications, Internet access, and internal connections services. See 47 U.S.C. 254(h). The program is administered by the Universal Service Administrative Company (USAC) pursuant to regulations promulgated by the Federal Communications Commission. See Federal Communications Commission, Universal Service for Schools and Libraries, available at *http://www.fcc.gov/wcb/universal_service/schoolsandlibs.html*.

According to USAC, approximately 82 percent of public schools and 10 percent of private schools received E-rate funding in the Fiscal Year (FY) 2000 funding cycle (July 1, 2000 through June 30, 2001) (using 1997 data base as denominator). See Universal Service Administrative Company, available at *http://www.sl.universolservice.org*. Public libraries also rely heavily on Erate funding; 57 percent of main public libraries received E-rate funding in FY 2000. *Id.; see also* LJ Budget Report 2002 supra.

In October 2000, Congress passed the Children's Internet Protection Act (CIPA) as part of the Consolidated Appropriations Act of 2001 (Pub. L. No. 106-554). Under section 1721 of the Act, schools and libraries that receive discounted telecommunications, Internet access, or internal connections services under the E-rate program are required to certify and adopt an Internet safety policy and to employ technological methods that block or filter certain visual depictions deemed obscene, pornographic, or harmful to minors for both minors and adults.[1] The Federal Communications Commission implemented the required changes to the E-rate program and the new CIPA certification requirements became effective for the fourth E-rate funding year that began on July 1, 2001, and ends on June 30, 2002. *See* Federal-State joint Board on Universal Service, Children's Internet Protection Act, *Report and Order, CC* Docket No. 96-45 (March 30, 2001), available *at http://www.fcc.gov/wcb/universal_service/schools andlibs.html.*

Section 1703(a) of CIPA directs NTIA to initiate a notice and comment proceeding to determine if currently available blocking and filtering technologies adequately address the needs of educational institutions, make recommendations on how to foster the development of technologies that meet the needs of schools and libraries, and evaluate current Internet safety policies. Section 1703(a) of CIPA specifically provides:

Sec 1703 Study of Technology Protection Measures

(a) IN GENERAL B Not later than 18 months after the date of the enactment of this Act, the National Telecommunications and Information Administration shall initiate a notice and comment proceeding for purposes of--

(1) Evaluating whether or not currently available technology protection measures, including commercial Internet blocking and filtering software, adequately address the needs of educational institutions;

(2) Making recommendations on how to foster the development of measures that meet such needs; and

(3) Evaluating the development and effectiveness of local Internet safety policies that are currently in operation after community input

Internet Blocking and Filtering Software and Acceptable Use Policies

The computer industry has developed a number of technology protection measures to block or filter prohibited content in response to the growing amount of online content. Among these measures are stand alone filters, monitoring software, and online parental controls.

---

[1] NITA notes that Sections 1712 and 1721 of the CHIP are currently the subject of constitutional challenge See American Library Assn v United States, No 01-CV-1303 (ED Pa March 20, 2001); Multnomah County Public Library v United States, No 01-CV-1322 (E D Pa March 20, 2001) NITA is not seeking comment on the constitutionality of the statute or its provisions

The Pew Internet and American Life Project reports that more than 41 percent (2 of every 5) of parents of children using the Internet rely on monitoring software or use pre-selected controls on their home computers. Pew Internet and American Life Project, The Internet and Education: Findings of the Pew Internet and American Life Project, at 5 (September 2001), available at *http://www.pewinternet.org/reports/toc.asp?Report=36.*
A Consumer Reports study indicated, however, that some technology protection companies refuse to disclose their method of blocking or filtering and their list of blocked sites, although users can submit Web addresses to check against blocked lists in some cases. See Digital Chaperones for Kids: Which Internet Filters Protect the Best? Which Get in the Way?, Consumer Reports at 2 (March 2001). Another report indicates that technology protection tools can require a fair amount of technical expertise in order to be manipulated successfully, such as an understanding of how to unblock sites, adjust tools for different levels of access, and examine and interpret log files. Trevor Shaw, What's Wrong with CIPA, E-School News (March 1, 2001), available at *http://www.eschoolnews.com/features/cipa/cipa3.cfm.*

The National Research Council (NRC) of the National Academy of Sciences recently released a report describing the social and educational strategies, technology-based tools, and legal and regulatory approaches to protect children from inappropriate material on the Internet. *See Youth, Pornography, and the Internet,* Committee to Study Tools and Strategies for Protecting Kids from Pornography and Their Applicability to Other Inappropriate Internet Content, National Research Council (NRC Report) (May 2, 2002), available at *http://bob.nap.edu/html/youth_internet/es.html.*

Among other things, the NRC Report concludes that perhaps the most important social and educational strategy for ensuring safe online experiences for children is responsible adult involvement and supervision. *Id.* at ES-7, 209. This strategy includes families, schools, libraries, and other organizations developing acceptable use policies to provide explicit guidelines about how individuals will conduct themselves online that will serve as a framework within which children can become more responsible for making better choices. *Id.* at 218. The Report notes that acceptable use policies are most effective when developed jointly with schools and communities. *Id.* at 219.

The Report suggests that acceptable use policies are not without problems, including how to avoid the "one size fits all" problem that may arise in trying to craft a policy that is appropriate for both young children as well as teenagers. *Id.* at 219-220. The NRC Report also discusses the ways that technology provides parents and other responsible adults with additional choices as to how best to protect children from inappropriate material on the Internet. *Id.* at ES-8, 255-304. The report notes, however, that filtering/ blocking tools are all imperfect in that they may "overblock" otherwise appropriate material or "underblock" some inappropriate material. *Id.* at 259-266.

Specific Questions

In an effort to enhance NTIA'S understanding of the present state of technology protection measures and Internet safety policies, NTIA solicits responses to the following questions. NTIA requests that interested parties submit written comments on any issue of fact, law, or policy that may provide information that is relevant to this evaluation. Commenters are invited to discuss any relevant issue, regardless of whether it is identified below. To the extent possible, please provide copies of studies, surveys, research, or other empirical data referenced in responses.

Evaluation of Available Technology Protection Measures

Section 1703(a)(1) of the Act requires NITA to evaluate whether or not currently available technology protection measures, including commercial Internet blocking and filtering software, adequately address the needs of educational institutions.

1. Discuss whether available technology protection measures adequately address the needs of educational institutions.

2. Is the use of particular technologies or procedures more prevalent than others?

3. What technology, procedure, or combination has had the most success within educational institutions?

4. Please explain how the technology protection products block or filter prohibited content (such as "yes" lists, (appropriate content); "no" lists, (prohibited content), human review, technology review based on phrase or image, or other method.) Explain whether these methods successfully block or filter prohibited online content and whether one method is more effective than another.

5. Are there obstacles to or difficulties in obtaining lists of blocked or filtered sites or the specific criteria used by technology companies to deny or permit access to certain web sites? Explain.

6. Do technology companies readily add or delete specific web sites from their blocked lists upon request? Please explain your answer.

7. Discuss any factors that were considered when deciding which technology tools to use (such as training, cost, technology maintenance and upgrades or other factors.)

Fostering the Development of Technology Measures

Section 1703(a)(2) directs NTIA to initiate a notice and comment proceeding to make recommendations on how to foster the development of technology measures that meet the needs of educational institutions,

1. Are current blocking and filtering methods effectively protecting children or limiting their access to prohibited Internet activity?

2. If technologies are available but are not used by educational institutions for other reasons, such as cost or training, please discuss.

3. What technology features would better meet the needs of educational institutions trying to block prohibited content?

4. Can currently available filtering or blocking technology adjust to accommodate all age groups from kindergarten through grade twelve? Are these tools easily disabled to accommodate bona fide and other lawful research? Are these tools easily dismantled?

Current Internet Safety Policies

Section 1703(a)(3) requires NTIA to evaluate the development and effectiveness of local Internet safety policies currently in operation that were established with community input.

1. Are Internet safety policies an effective method of filtering or blocking prohibited material consistent with the goals established by educational institutions and the community? If not, please discuss the areas in which the policies do not effectively meet the goals of the educational institutions and/or community.

2. Please discuss whether and how the current policies could better meet the needs of the institutions and the community. If possible, provide specific recommendations.

3. Are educational institutions using a single technology protection method or a combination of blocking and filtering technologies?

4. Describe any best practices or policies that have been effective in ensuring that minors are protected from exposure to prohibited content. Please share practices proven unsuccessful at protecting minors from exposure to prohibited content.

Dated: May 22, 2002

Kathy D Smith,

Chief Counsel, National Telecommunications and

Information Administration

[FR Doc 02-13286 Filed 5-28-02; 8:45 am]

Appendix II: List of Commenters

American Center for Law and Justice (ACLJ)
American Civil Liberties Union (ACLU)
American Library Association
Center for Democracy and Technology (CDT)
Cleanweb.net
Charles M. Bailey Public Library, Winthrop, Maine Consortium for School Networking
DoBox, Inc.
David Duggan
e-Mints
East Brunswick Public Library, East Brunswick, NJ
Electronic Privacy Information Center (EPIC)
Evanston Public Library, Evanston, Illinois
Seth Finkelstein
Florida Gulf Coast University
Fort Morgan Public Library, Fort Morgan, Colorado
Free Expression Policy Project (FEPP)
Grayson County Public Library
Daniel S. Hahn
International Society for Technology in Education (ISTE)
Jefferson-Lewis BOCHES
Joseph McClane
Leo L. Mosier
Kidsnet, Inc.
Las Vegas-Clark County Library District
Meadowbrook High School Library
Mid-Atlantic Regional Technology in Education Consortium (MAR*TEC)
Morality in Media (MIM)
N2H2, Inc.
National Education Association (NEA)
Palo Alto United School District, Palo Alto, California
Rebecca Ramsby
Responsible Netizen Institute (Nancy Willard)
St. Pius X School, Urbana, Iowa
Vericept Corporation
Kristen Wallace
WiredSafety.org (Parry Aftab)

Appendix III: Filtering Effectiveness Tests Cited in *N2H2 Comments to the NTIA*

Test	Date	Product	Effectiveness	Method
PC Week	4/7/1995	Websense	Mixed	Query sample of URLs
PC Magazine	11/7/1995	CyberSitter	Mixed	Query sample of URLs
PC Magazine	11/7/1995	Net Nanny	Ineffective	Query sample of URLs
PC Magazine	11/7/1995	SurfWatch	Mixed	Query sample of URLs
Internet World	9/1/1996	Cyber Patrol	Effective	Query sample of URLs
Internet World	9/1/1996	CyberSitter	Mixed	Query sample of URLs
Internet World	9/1/1996	InterGo	Effective	Query sample of URLs
Internet World	9/1/1996	Net Nanny	Ineffective	Query sample of URLs
Internet World	9/1/1996	Net Shepherd	Mixed	Query sample of URLs
Internet World	9/1/1996	Specs for Kids	Effective	Query sample of URLs
Internet World	9/1/1996	SurfWatch	Mixed	Query sample of URLs
PC Magazine	4/8/1997	Cyber Patrol	Effective	Query sample of URLs
PC Magazine	4/8/1997	CyberSitter	Effective	Query sample of URLs
PC Magazine	4/8/1997	CyberSnoop	Effective	Query sample of URLs
PC Magazine	4/8/1997	Net Nanny	Effective	Query sample of URLs
PC Magazine	4/8/1997	Rated PG	Effective	Query sample of URLs
PC Magazine	4/8/1997	SurfWatch	Effective	Query sample of URLs
PC Magazine	4/8/1997	X-Stop	Effective	Query sample of URLs
Consumer Reports	5/1/1997	Cyber Patrol	Ineffective	Query sample of URLs
Consumer Reports	5/1/1997	CyberSitter	Ineffective	Query sample of URLs
Consumer Reports	5/1/1997	Net Nanny	Ineffective	Query sample of URLs
Consumer Reports	5/1/1997	SurfWatch	Ineffective	Query sample of URLs
PC Magazine	5/6/1997	Little Brother	Effective	Query sample of URLs
PC Magazine	5/6/1997	ON Guard	Effective	Query sample of URLs
PC Magazine	5/6/1997	SmartFilter	Effective	Query sample of URLs
PC Magazine	5/6/1997	SurfWatch	Effective	Query sample of URLs
PC Magazine	5/6/1997	Websense	Effective	Query sample of URLs
InfoWorld	8/18/1997	Websense	Effective	Query sample of URLs
PC World	10/1/1997	Cyber Patrol	Mixed	Query sample of URLs
PC World	10/1/1997	CyberSitter	Effective	Query sample of URLs
PC World	10/1/1997	Net Nanny	Mixed	Query sample of URLs
PC World	10/1/1997	Net Shepherd	Mixed	Query sample of URLs
PC World	10/1/1997	SurfWatch	Effective	Query sample of URLs
Computer Shopper	11/1/1997	CyberSitter	Effective	Query sample of URLs
MacWorld	11/1/1997	Cyber Patrol	Effective	Query sample of URLs
MacWorld	11/1/1997	SurfWatch	Effective	Query sample of URLs
MacWorld	11/1/1997	X-Stop	Effective	Query sample of URLs
Internet Magazine	12/1/1997	Cyber Patrol	Effective	Query sample of URLs
Internet Magazine	12/1/1997	Cyber Snoop	Effective	Query sample of URLs
Internet Magazine	12/1/1997	CyberSitter	Effective	Query sample of URLs
Internet Magazine	12/1/1997	N2H2	Effective	Query sample of URLs
Internet Magazine	12/1/1997	SafeSurf	Effective	Query sample of URLs
Internet Magazine	12/1/1997	SurfWatch	Effective	Query sample of URLs
Internet Magazine	12/1/1997	Websense	Effective	Query sample of URLs
Internet Magazine	12/1/1997	X-Stop	Effective	Query sample of URLs
InfoWorld	2/16/1998	Cyber Sentinel	Effective	Query sample of URLs
PC Magazine	3/24/1998	Cyber Patrol	Effective	Query sample of URLs
PC Magazine	3/24/1998	Cyber Sentinel	Effective	Query sample of URLs
PC Magazine	3/24/1998	Cyber Sitter	Effective	Query sample of URLs

Appendix IV: Sample Acceptable Use Policies

1. Fairfax County Public Schools

Acceptable Use Policy for Network Access

> *The information systems and Internet access available through FCPS are available to support learning, enhance instruction, and support school system business practices.*

FCPS information systems are operated for the mutual benefit of all users. The use of the FCPS Network is a privilege, not a right. Users should not do, or attempt to do, anything that might disrupt the operation of the network or equipment and/or interfere with the learning of other students or work of other FCPS employees. The FCPS Network is connected to the Internet, a network of networks, which enables people to interact with hundreds of thousands of networks and computers.

All access to the FCPS Network shall be preapproved by the principal or program manager. The school or office may restrict or terminate any user's access, without prior notice, if such action is deemed necessary to maintain computing availability and security for other users of the systems. Other disciplinary action may be imposed as stated in the Fairfax County Public Schools Student Responsibilities and Rights (SR&R) document.

Respect for Others

Users should respect the rights of others using the FCPS Network by:

- Using assigned workstations as directed by the teacher.
- Being considerate when using scarce resources.
- Always logging off workstations after finishing work.
- Not deliberately attempting to disrupt system performance or interfere with the work of other users.
- Leaving equipment and room in good condition for the next user or class.

Ethical Conduct for Users

Accounts on the FCPS Network, both school-based and central, are considered private, although absolute security of any data cannot be guaranteed. It is the responsibility of the user to:

- Use only his or her account or password. It is a violation to give access to an account to any other user.
- Recognize and honor the intellectual property of others; comply with legal restrictions regarding plagiarism and the use and citation of information resources.
- Not read, modify, or remove files owned by other users.
- Restrict the use of the FCPS Network and resources to the mission or function of the school system. The use of the FCPS Network for personal use or for private gain is prohibited.
- Help maintain the integrity of the school information system. Deliberate tampering or experimentation is not allowed, which includes the use of FCPS Network and resources to illicitly access, tamper with, or experiment with systems outside FCPS.

Respect for Property

The only software, other than students' projects, to be used on school computers or the school network are those products that the school may legally use. Copying copyrighted software without full compliance with terms of a preauthorized licensing agreement is a serious federal offense and will not be tolerated. Modifying any copyrighted software or borrowing software is not permitted.

- Do not modify or rearrange keyboards, individual key caps, monitors, printers, or any other peripheral equipment.
- Report equipment problems immediately to teacher or program manager.
- Leave workstations and peripherals in their designated places.

Appropriate Use

- Do not use offensive, obscene, or harassing language when using any FCPS Network system.
- Information may not be posted if it: violates the privacy of others, jeopardizes the health and safety of students, is obscene or libelous, causes disruption of school activities, plagiarizes the work of others, is a commercial advertisement, or is not approved by the principal or program manager.
- Users will not change or delete files belonging to others.
- Real-time messaging and online chat may only be used with the permission of the teacher or program manager.
- Students are not to reveal personal information (last name, home address, phone number) in correspondence with unknown parties.
- Users exercising their privilege to use the Internet as an educational resource shall accept the responsibility for all material they receive.
- Users are prohibited from accessing portions of the Internet that do not promote the instructional mission of FCPS.
- All student-produced web pages are subject to approval and ongoing review by responsible teacher and/or principal. All web pages should reflect the mission and character of the school.

Related Documents: *Student Responsibilities and Rights;* Regulation 6410.2

DECLARATION OF UNDERSTANDING AND ADHERENCE

I, the parent or guardian of _____ (student's name), the minor student who has signed, along with me, this acceptable use policy, understand that my son or daughter must adhere to the terms of this policy. I understand that access to the FCPS Network is designed for educational purposes but will also allow my son or daughter access to external computer databases, networks, etc. that are not controlled by FCPS. I also understand that some materials available through these external sources may be inappropriate and objectionable; however, I acknowledge that it is impossible for FCPS to screen or review all of the materials available through these sources. I accept responsibility to set and convey standards for appropriate and acceptable use to my son or daughter when he or she is using the FCPS Network or any other electronic media or communications associated with FCPS.

_____   _____   _____
Date   Parent or Guardian Name (Please Print)   Parent or Guardian Signature

_____   _____
Student Name (Please Print)   Student Signature

2. Lake Washington School District

LAKE WASHINGTON SCHOOL DISTRICT
Computer Equipment Appropriate Use Procedures

PURPOSE

The Lake Washington School District provides a wide range of computer resources to its students and staff for the purpose of advancing the educational mission of the District. These resources are provided and maintained at the District's -- and therefore, the public's --expense and are to be used by members of the school community with respect for the public trust through which they have been provided.

The Appropriate Use Procedures that follow provide details regarding the appropriate and inappropriate use of District computers. The procedures do not attempt to articulate all required or proscribed behavior by users. Successful operation of the District computer network requires that all users conduct themselves in a responsible, decent, ethical, and polite manner while using the District computers. You, the user, are ultimately responsible for your actions in accessing and using District computers and the District computer network. As a user of District computers, you are expected to review and understand the guidelines and procedures in this document.

APPROPRIATE USE PROCEDURES

Scope

The following procedures apply to all District staff and students, and covers all District computer equipment including any desktop or laptop computers provided to staff, the District computer network ("LWSDNet"), and any computer software licensed to the District ("District Computers").

Appropriate Use

The District expects everyone to exercise good judgment and use the computer equipment in a professional manner. Your use of the equipment is expected to be related to the District's goals of educating students and/or conducting District business. The District recognizes, however, that some personal use is inevitable, and that incidental and occasional personal use that is infrequent or brief in duration is permitted so long as it occurs on personal time, does not interfere with District business, and is not otherwise prohibited by District policy or procedures.

Use of District Software: District software is licensed to the District by a large number of vendors and may have specific license restrictions regarding copying or using a particular program. Users of District software must obtain permission from the District prior to copying or loading District software onto *any* computer, whether the computer is privately owned or is a District Computer.

Use of Non-District Software: Prior to loading non-District software onto District Computers (including laptops, desktops, and LWSDNet), a user must receive permission from the District. The District will create a list of "authorized software" programs that may be loaded onto District laptops without specific permission. For example, a user will be able to load software onto a laptop that is necessary for a user to access a personal Internet service for the purpose of remotely accessing the District's email network. **All software must be legally licensed by the user prior to loading onto District Equipment.** The unauthorized use of and/or copying of software is illegal,

> *"It is against LWSD practice for staff or students to copy or reproduce any licensed software on LWSD computing equipment, except as expressly permitted by the specific software license. Unauthorized use of software is regarded as a serious matter and any such use is without the consent of L WSD."*
> ***LSWD Directive 1/29/1990***

Remote Access: The District provides remote access to its internal email network for the convenience of its staff. Users may access the District's email network over a standard Internet connection by using either a District laptop or a privately-owned computer. District laptops also have the ability to use the District's email network "off-line." A user's email folders are stored locally on the laptop. Therefore, a user may read, delete, and reply to District email, and create new email, without a direct connection to the network. Any reply or new email created by the user will be sent to the recipient the next time the user connects to the network. Also, at the time of the direct connection to the network, email delivered while the user was off-line will be immediately downloaded to the laptop.

Prohibited Uses: District Computers may not be used for the following purposes:

- *Commercial Use:* Using District Computers for personal or private gain, personal business, or commercial advantage is prohibited.

- *Political Use:* Using District Computers for political purposes in violation of federal, state, or local laws is prohibited. This prohibition includes using District computers to assist or to advocate, directly or indirectly, for or against a ballot proposition and/or the election of any person to any office. The use of District Computers for the expression of personal political opinions to elected officials is prohibited. Only those staff authorized by the Superintendent may express the District's position on pending legislation or other policy matters.

- *Illegal or Indecent Use:* Using District Computers for illegal, harassing, vandalizing, inappropriate, or indecent purposes (including accessing, storing, or viewing pornographic, indecent, or otherwise inappropriate material), or in support of such activities is prohibited. Illegal activities are any violations of federal, state, or local laws (for example, copyright infringement, publishing defamatory information, or committing fraud). Harassment includes slurs, comments, jokes, innuendoes, unwelcome compliments, cartoons, pranks, or verbal conduct relating to an individual that (1) have the purpose or effect or creating and intimidating, a hostile or offensive environment; (2) have the purpose or effect of unreasonably interfering with an individual's work or school performance, or (3) interfere with school operations. Vandalism is any attempt to harm or destroy the operating system, application software, or data. Inappropriate use includes any violation of the purpose and goal of the network. Indecent activities include violations of generally accepted social standards for use of publicly-owned and operated equipment.

- *Non-District Employee Use:* District Computers may only be used by District staff and students, and others expressly authorized by the District to use the equipment.

- *Disruptive Use:* District Computers may not be used to interfere or disrupt other users, services, or equipment. For example, disruptions 'include distribution of unsolicited advertising ("Spam"), propagation of computer viruses, distribution of large quantities of information that may overwhelm the system (chain letters, network games, or broadcasting messages), and any unauthorized access to or destruction of District Computers or other resources accessible through the District's computer network ("Crack Mug" or "Hacking").

Privacy

District Computers, the Internet, and use of email are not inherently secure or private. For example, the content of an email message, including attachments, is most analogous to a letter or official memo rather than a telephone call, since a record of the contents of the email may be preserved by the sender, recipient, any parties to whom the email may be forwarded, or by the email system itself. It is important to remember that once an email message is sent, the sender has no control over where it may be forwarded and deleting a message from the user's computer system does not necessarily delete it from the District computer system. In some cases, emails have also been treated as public records in response to a public records disclosure request. Likewise, files, such as Internet "cookies" (explained more fully below) may be created and stored on a computer without the user's knowledge. **Users are urged to be caretaker's of your own privacy and to not store sensitive or personal information on District Computers.** The District may need to access, monitor, or review electronic data stored on District Computers, including email and Internet usage records.

While the District respects the privacy of its staff and while the District currently does not have a practice of monitoring or reviewing electronic information, the District reserves the right to do so for any reason. The District may monitor and review the information in order to analyze the use of systems or compliance with policies, conduct audits, review performance or conduct, obtain information, or for other reasons. The District reserves the right to disclose any electronic message to law enforcement officials, and under some circumstances, may be required to disclose information to law enforcement officials, the public, or other third parties, for example, in response to a document production request made in a lawsuit involving the District or by a third party against the user or pursuant to a public records disclosure request.

Discipline

The Appropriate Use Procedures are applicable to all users of District Computers and refers to all information resources whether 'individually controlled, shared, stand alone, or networked. Disciplinary action, if any, for students, staff, and other users shall be consistent with the District's standard policies and practices. Violations may constitute cause for revocation of access privileges, suspension of access to District computers, other school disciplinary action, and/or appropriate legal action. Specific disciplinary measures will be determined on a case-by-case basis.

<u>Care for District Computer</u>

Users of District Computers are expected to respect the District's property and be responsible in using the equipment. Users are to follow any District instructions regarding maintenance or care of the equipment. Users may be held responsible for any damage caused by your intentional or negligent acts in caring for District Computers under your control. The District is responsible for any routine maintenance or standard repairs to District Computers. Users are expected to timely notify the District of any need for service.

Users are not to delete or add software to District Computers without District permission. Due to different licensing terms for different software programs, it is not valid to assume that if it is permissible to copy one program, then it is permissible to copy others.

If a District laptop is lost, damaged, or stolen while under the control of a user, the user is expected to file a daim under his/her insurance coverage, where coverage is available. Except in cases of negligent or intentional loss or damage, the District will cover out-of-pocket expenses.

USING EMAIL AND THE INTERNET WISELY

<u>Using Email Wisely</u>

- Email encourages informal communication because it is easy to use. However, unlike a telephone call however, email creates a permanent record that is archived and often transmitted to others. Remember that even when you delete an email from your mailbox, it still may exist in the system for some period of time.

- Be circumspect about what you send and to whom. Do not say anything in an email that you would not want to see republished throughout the District, in Internet email, or on the front page of the *Eastside Journal*. Remember that email invites sharing; a push of the button will re-send your message worldwide, if any recipient (or hacker) decides to do so. What you say can be republished and stored by others.

- Beware of the "Reply All" button. Often your message only needs to be returned to one individual -- is the message really appropriate for (and should it really take the time of) everyone on the address list?

- You can create liability for yourself and the District. For example, within or outside the District, if you "publish" (type or re-send) words that defame another individual or disparage another individual or institution, if you upload or download or re-send copyrighted or pornographic material, if you use email to harass or discriminate against someone, or if you send private information or data about someone, you may violate applicable laws and District policy. Make sure none of your activities violate any law or policy.

- Please keep in mind that because of intermediary server problems and other potential delays, Internet email can sometimes take anywhere from five minutes to several days to arrive. It may not be the best means to send time-sensitive information.

- Finally, beware of sending attachments. They may arrive garbled if the recipient is using a different email system.

- Email attachments can introduce viruses into the District system, and you can introduce a virus into a recipient's system by forwarding an infected attachment. This is especially likely if the attachment arrives from an unknown source via the Internet. If you do not know the sender of Internet email, consider routing the message to the MIS staff who can open the attachment for you on a computer isolated from the District network. While that should prevent activating a virus, it will not stop certain other infections (e.g., a logic bomb). Please do not open attached files ending in 46EXE,99 "BAT," or "COM," as these files may be viruses or programs designed to delete data from the computer.

Using the Internet Access Wisely

- Be circumspect about where you go and what you do. Do not visit any site or download or share any material that might cause anyone to question your professionalism, or the District's.

- Read the "License" or "Legal" contract terms on every site. Do not purport to bind the District to any license or other contract. If you make an agreement on your own behalf, do not violate that agreement using the District equipment or Internet account. Do not assume that just because something is on the Internet, you may copy i. As a general rule, assume that everything is copyrighted and do not copy it unless there is a notice on the site stating that you may do so. For example, if you see a clever cartoon assume that you may NOT copy it. Governmental documents are an exception (you may copy them), but you must confirm that it is the "government" and not a government-related entity such as the post office.

- Be aware of the "Do you want a cookie?" messages (if you have configured your browser to get such messages). If you answer yes, whatever activity in which you are engaged will be logged by the site owner to help it or its advertisers develop a profile about you or the District. It is possible that your browser is set to accept cookies without asking you each time.

- You can create liability for yourself and the District. For example, if you "publish" (type or re-send) words that defame or disparage another individual or institution, if you upload or download or re-send copyrighted or pornographic material, if you use the Internet to harass or discriminate against someone, or if you provide private information or data about someone, you may violate applicable laws or District policy. Make sure none of your activities violate any law or policy.

- Do not engage in any "spamming" or other activities that could clog or congest Internet networks.